FLUTE EDITIO

BOOK ONE

Band

Expressions™

Band Expressions Author Team

Co-Lead Author: Robert W. Smith

Co-Lead Author: Susan L. Smith

Michael Story   Garland E. Markham   Richard C. Crain

Contributor: Linda J. Gammon

Percussion Contributor: James Campbell

Art Credits: page 5, *Butterfly II* by Paul Giovanopoulos, ©1995 Paul Giovanopoulos c/o Theispot Showcase;
page 34, *Scenes of Daily Life in Korea* by Kim Junkeun, ©Christies Images Ltd. 1995;
page 38, *Celebration 1975* by Charles Searles, ©Smithsonian American Art Musuem, Washington D.C./Art Resource, NY.

Expressions Music Curriculum™, Music Expressions™, Band Expressions™, Jazz Expressions™,
Orchestra Expressions™, Choral Expressions™, Piano Expressions™, and Guitar Expressions™
are trademarks of Warner Bros. Publications. All Rights Reserved.

1 2 3 4 5 6 7 8 9 10   10 09 08 07 06 05 04 03
© 2003 WARNER BROS. PUBLICATIONS U.S. INC.
All Rights Reserved

Warner Bros. Publications • 15800 NW 48th Avenue • Miami, FL 33014

The Art of Playing

Instrument and Parts

Foot Joint   **Middle Joint**   **Head Joint**

(D Key)   **Embouchure Hole**

Assembly Procedure

1. Place the head joint into the middle joint by gently twisting. Make sure the embouchure hole lines up with the first key of the middle joint.

2. Gently twist the foot joint onto the middle joint lining it up with the center of the D hole.

Disassembly Procedure

1. Remove the head joint and the foot joint.

2. Swab each part with a cloth tucked into the cleaning rod.

3. Gently wipe off the outside of the keys with a soft cloth.

4. Place your instrument carefully in the case and close all latches completely.

5. Cases are for your instrument only, not for music, folders, or books.

Care and Maintenance

- Keep the flute clean and free of moisture by swabbing after each use with a small cleaning cloth tucked into the cleaning rod.

- Gently wipe the outside of the keys with a soft cloth each time before returning the flute to the case.

- Always place the flute down on a chair resting with the keys facing upward.

- Avoid resting the flute on the lip of a music stand.

- Take your instrument to a professional shop once a year for maintenance.

The Art of Playing

Rest Position

Ready Position

Play Position

Posture and Hand Position

- Sit toward the front of the chair with your feet flat on the floor.

- Position your upper body so that it is straight and relaxed as if you were standing.

- Hold the flute almost horizontal, close to a 90-degree angle.

- Form your right hand into a flat C with the thumb under the first and second fingers. Support the flute with your thumb and little finger.

- Rest the body of the flute on the base joint of the left hand index finger with the thumb touching the B key and fourth finger touching the G# key.

- Fingers should be curved and relaxed on top of the keys.

Embouchure Formation

1. Draw the corners of your mouth slightly back but not down, keeping your face soft.

2. Make your upper lip firm while keeping your lower lip soft.

3. Center your embouchure over the embouchure hole covering approximately one third of the opening.

4. Check with a mirror.

Supplies

- Tuning rod with small cloth.
- Soft cloth
- Metronome
- Pencil
- Small mirror
- Wire music stand

Creative Tools of Music (Units 2 and 3)

Articulation—a slight interruption of the air stream with the tongue

Bar Line—a vertical line placed on a staff to divide music into measures

Breath Mark—a recommended place to breathe

Clef—placed at the beginning of the staff to identify the note names

Embouchure—the natural formation of the facial and lip muscles on the mouthpiece or reed

Fermata—hold the note or rest longer than note value

Final Bar Line—indicates the end of a piece of music

Flat—lowers the pitch of a note one half step

Grand Staff—treble and bass clef staves joined together

Interval—the distance between two pitches

Ledger Lines—short lines placed above or below the staff

Measure—the space between two bar lines to form a grouping of beats

Musical Alphabet—the letter names of the notes used in music

Rhythm—the organization of sound and silence in time

Sharp—raises the pitch of a note one half step

Staff—5 lines and 4 spaces on which notes are placed

Time Signature—a symbol placed at the beginning of the staff indicating the number of beats per measure and what kind of note gets one beat

4/4   4 beats per measure quarter note recieves one beat

Musical Alphabet Games

Air Stream   Inhale   E x h a l e   Inhale
(1 2 3 4)   (1   2   3   4)   (1 2 3 4)

Band @ Home

LESSON 1
1. Teach one or more of your family members how to inhale and exhale in order to play a wind instrument.
2. Time how long you and your family members can exhale against a piece of paper.

LESSON 2
1. Demonstrate to your family the following:
   • Instrument assembly
   • Rest/Ready/Play positions
   • Instrument disassembly
2. Complete the Instrument Parts and Assembly Procedure worksheet and bring it to our next class.

LESSON 3
1. Practice assembling and disassembling your instrument.
2. Create a variety of rhythms to sing with the recording of "One Note Rock" using the syllable "toh" or "doh."   CD :4

Butterfly II, by Paul Giovanopoulos

©1995 Paul Giovanopoulos c/o Theispot Showcase

1 *First Sounds*

Set	Ready	Breathe	F ——————————————→
1	2	(3 4)	

2 *Mouthpiece Rock* CD :5

—— Play two times ——

Set	Ready	Breathe
1	2	(3 4)

F → | R e s t | F → | R e s t |

1 2 3 4 1 2 (3 4) 1 2 3 4 1 2 (3 4)

3 *First Note* CD :6

Set	Ready	Breathe
1	2	(3 4)

4 *One Note Shout* CD :7

—— Play two times ——

Set	Ready	Breathe
1	2	(3 4)

Rest   Rest

1 2 3 4   1 2 (3 4)   1 2 3 4   1 2 (3 4)

5 *One Note Reggae* CD :8

Set	Ready	Breathe
1	2	(3 4)

F —————→ | F → | F → | F F F F | Rest —————→

go to next line

1 2 3 4   1 2 3 4   1 2 3 4   1 2 3 4

F —————————→ | F F F F | F —→ | F —→ | F —→ | Rest →

1 2 3 4   1 2 3 4   1 2 3 4   1 2 3 4

Band @ Home

LESSON 1

1. Practice "Mouthpiece Rock" with the recorded accompaniment.

2. Demonstrate for your family how to produce the first sounds on your mouthpiece.

3. Perform "Mouthpiece Rock" with the accompaniment track for your family.

LESSON 2

1. Practice forming your embouchure. Remember—it is important that you practice bringing the mouthpiece to your embouchure to become more comfortable with producing these first sounds.

2. Sustain your first tone on F as long as possible while keeping the air stream and tone steady. Be sure to focus and "energize" your air stream.

3. Perform "One Note Shout" with the accompaniment track for your family and/or friends.

LESSON 3

1. Sustain a steady sound over 8 to 12 counts.

2. Practice your first note and articulation by playing "One Note Reggae." Practice your "toe-tap" with a steady beat while articulating the quarter notes.

3. Show your family and/or friends the graphic *Butterfly II* and explain the groupings of "4." Perform "One Note Reggae" for your family and/or friends and read *Butterfly II* as your music.

4. Create your own graphic that represents patterns of quarter notes and quarter rests.

UNIT 4

Creative Tools of Music

Critique—an evaluation of the quality of a performance

 Ledger Lines—short lines placed above or below the staff for pitches beyond the range of the staff

Fermata—hold the note (or rest) longer than the note value

Rest—a silent unit of time.

Intonation—the accuracy of pitch or pitch relationships in the performance of music

Soli—a line of music played by a small group of instruments

Tutti—all play

- Light blue highlights indicate new notes.
- Light yellow highlights indicate new rhythms.
- Light red highlights indicate new terms and symbols.

$\frac{4}{4}$ = 4 beats in a measure
Quarter note gets one beat

6 Learning Our First Note

Quarter note = ♩ = 1 beat

Quarter rest = 𝄽 = 1 beat

7 Quarter Note Rock CD :9

8 Fermata Warm-Up CD :10

9 More Quarters CD :11

6

10 **Soli Jam** CD :12

11 **My Quarters**

12 **New Notes**

13 **El Toro** CD :13

These are flat, too.

Band @ Home

LESSON 1

1. Practice "More Quarters" for our next lesson. This exercise will help you develop your music reading skills.

LESSON 2

1. Schedule a consistent, daily time for practice in a quiet place so you are not distracted and can focus entirely on your music.

2. Practice "New Notes." This exercise introduces two new notes for your instrument. Notice the fingering chart in your book for the new notes.

3. Play "New Notes" for your family to show them what you have been learning.

4. Compose your own piece on the line entitled "My Quarters" in your book. Use any combination of quarter notes and quarter rests on your first note for the eight-measure composition. Be prepared to perform your composition in our next class.

LESSON 3

1. Practice "Mixing the Three" in Unit 5.

2. Explore www.band-expressions.com to find out more information about music and your instrument.

UNIT 5

Creative Tools of Music

Canon—a technique to compose music in which the melody is introduced in one voice and echoed by another voice

Solo—a performance by one person playing alone, with or without accompaniment

14 Mixing the Three

These are flat, too

15 Solo Rock CD :14

These are flat, too   Solo   tutti

16 Creative Expression

17 Going the Distance

These are flat, too

18 Hymnsong CD :15

These are flat, too

19 *Putting It Together*

These are flat, too   Solo   tutti

20 **Round and Round We Go**

These are flat, too

21 *Canon Roll*

Creative Tools Notation

Band @ Home

LESSON 1

1. Remember—it is important to follow our daily practice routine.

2. Practice "Going the Distance." This challenging exercise reviews what we have already learned.

LESSON 2

1. Practice "Putting it Together." This selection reviews what we have learned to this point.

2. Remember the importance of the daily practice routine to build endurance.

LESSON 3

1. Compose and teach a family member a canon using body percussion.

2. Be prepared to teach your canon to the band in our next lesson.

3. On the "Creative Tools Notation" line, practice drawing your clef, time signature, barlines, quarter notes and rests, a fermata, and a final barline.

Creative Tools of Music

Balance—all parts played and heard equally

Duet—a piece of music with two interacting parts

Harmony—the result of two or more tones sounded at the same time

Key—the tonality of a piece of music

Key Signature—flats or sharps placed at the beginning of the staff that indicate which notes are to be altered throughout the piece

March—music for a parade or procession

Musical Line—direction or shape of a musical thought or ideaa

Unison—all performers play the same note

22 Three Note Warm-Up

23 Woodchopper's Ball CD :17

Words and Music by
JOE BISHOP and WOODY HERMAN

24 Two for the Show (Duet)

25 Two Tone Workout

26 Woodchopper's Ball (C Version) CD :19

Words and Music by
JOE BISHOP and WOODY HERMAN

27 A "Rock" Nophobia (Duet)
(The Eentsy Weentsy Spider)

Traditional, U.S.A.

These are flat, too

These are flat, too

28 Heroes March (Duet) CD :20

March

These are flat, too

This is flat, too

This is flat, too

29 Balance Our Sound (Duet)

This is flat, too

This is flat, too

This is flat, too

30 Ode to Joy (Duet) CD :21

LUDWIG VAN BEETHOVEN, Germany

Band @ Home

LESSON 1

1. Practice playing the new note we learned today.

2. Perform "Woodchopper's Ball" with the accompaniment CD for your family and friends.

LESSON 2

1. Play the new note for your family. Demonstrate your ability to hold and control steady long tones/beats.

2. Play 'Heroes March" with the CD accompaniment for your family and friends.

LESSON 3

1. Practice long tones on B♭ and C. Play both of these notes for four counts with four beats of rest between these two pitches.

2. Perform "Ode to Joy" with the accompaniment track for your family and friends.

3. Explore www.band-expressions.com to discover more information about music and your instrument.

UNIT 7

Creative Tools of Music

Chorale—a slow, "hymn-like" composition

Composer—a person who writes music

Phrase—a musical sentence or statement

 Repeat sign—symbol that indicates to go back and play the section of music again

PORTRAIT

John Williams

One of the most popular and successful American orchestral composers of the modern age, John Williams is the winner of five Academy Awards, 17 Grammys, three Golden Globes, and two Emmys. Mr. Williams has composed the music and served as music director for nearly eighty movies, including "Jaws;" "E.T.: The Extra-Terrestrial;" "Hook;" the "Indiana Jones;" trilogy and the "Star Wars" series. He is the Laureate Conductor of the Boston Pops Orchestra, which he conducted for 13 years and currently holds the title of Artist-in-Residence at Tanglewood, Massachusetts. He may be best known for the music he has written for the Olympics, including the well-known "Olympic Fanfare."

Whole note = o = 4 counts		Half note = ♩ = 2 counts
Whole rest = ▬ = 4 counts		Half rest = ▬ = 2 counts

31 *Echo Warm-Up*

32 *Whole Lotta Fun*

33 *Half the Time*

34 *Thanksgiving Song*

Folk Song, England

35 *Celebration* CD :22

Words and Music by
RONALD BELL, CLAYDES SMITH, GEORGE BROWN, JAMES TAYLOR,
ROBERT MICKENS, EARL TOON, DENNIS THOMAS, ROBERT BELL and EUMIR DEODATO

36 *Whole Note Warm-Up*

37 *Phrase Phun*

Phrase

38 OK Chorale (Duet)

39 All Through the Night

Folk Song, Wales

40 Augie's Great Municipal Band (Duet) CD :23

Music by
JOHN WILLIAMS

41 Theme From "Jaws"

Music by JOHN WILLIAMS

42 Creative Expression

Band @ Home

LESSON 1

1. Practice playing a whole note followed by a whole rest on each of the five notes we have learned so far.

2. Practice playing a half note followed by a half rest on each of the five notes.

3. Practice "Celebration" with the accompaniment.

LESSON 2

1. Practice the melodies we learned today.

Try to play two measures before taking a breath to create a phrase.

2. Time how many seconds you can sustain a note while maintaining a steady sound.

LESSON 3

1. Practice the song "Jaws."

2. On line 42, compose your own shark song using the notes you have learned so far. Experiment with soft and loud and fast and slow to create different types of sharks. What type of shark are you?

3. Perform the shark song you create for your family and friends. You may have the opportunity to perform your song for the class in our next lesson.

4. Ask your family or friends to name a piece by John Williams. If they do not know any of his works, tell them about the music you heard or played in class. (Star Wars, Jaws, E.T., etc.)

5. Perform "Augie's Great Municipal Band" and "Jaws" for your family and friends.

UNIT 8 IS PRESENTED BY YOUR TEACHER

UNIT 9

Creative Tools of Music

UNIT 8 IS PRESENTED BY YOUR TEACHER

Anacrusis—one or more notes that occur as a lead-in to the first full measure

Dynamics—musical performace levels of loud and soft

Sight-reading—reading and performing a piece of music for the first time

Subdivide—dividing a note into smaller sections or fractions

Dynamic Markings

p	the symbol for piano, meaning to play soft
mp	the symbol for mezzo piano, meaning to play medium soft
mf	the symbol for mezzo forte, meaning to play medium loud
f	the symbol for forte, meaning to play loud

43 **Playing the Phrase** CD :24

44 **Reading the Eighths**

45 **Three Pairs and a Caterpillar**

46 **Rain, Rain Go Away** CD :25

Traditional

47 **Creative Expression**

48 **Feel the Force!** CD :26

mf   *f*   *p*   *mf*   *f*

49 **Chitty, Chitty Bang Bang** CD :27

Words and Music by
RICHARD M. SHERMAN and ROBERT B. SHERMAN

f   *mf*   *f*   *mf*   *f*

14

This Arrangement © 2003 EMI Unart Catalog Inc.   All Rights Reserved

50 *Arre, Mi Burrito!* CD :28

Folk Song, Latin America

f   *p*

51 *Juba*

African-American Folk Song, U.S.A.

52 *Mary's New Groove* CD :29

Traditional, U.S.A.

mf

53 *Duerme Pronto* CD :30

Folk Song, Spain

mf   *p*

54 *Long Legged Sailor*

Traditional, Folk Song

mf

55 *Bang the Drum All Day* CD :31
(I Don't Want to Work)

Words and Music by TODD RUNDGREN

mf

I   don't want to work,   just   want   to   bang   on   the   drum   all   day.

I   don't want to work,   just   want   to   bang   on   the   drum   all   day.

Band @ Home

LESSON 1

1. Remember to follow your warm-up procedure. Play one of your favorite songs from earlier in the book to complete your warm-up.

2. On the Creative Expression line, create and notate four measures of eighth note and quarter note combinations using any pitch you can read and play. Clap, count, and play your composition.

3. Practice "Rain Rain, Go Away" with the CD accompaniment.

LESSON 2

1. Play the new song "Juba."

2. Draw dynamic symbols (piano, forte, mezzo forte, and mezzo piano) where you think they belong.

3. Play "Juba" with the dynamics you have added. Be prepared to play this in class next time.

4. Memorize "Rain, Rain Go Away."

LESSON 3

1. Teach the words to "Bang the Drum All Day" to your family and friends. Invite them to perform "Bang the Drum All Day" with you and the accompaniment track.

UNIT 10

Creative Tools of Music

Melody—a series of musical tones that form a recognizable phrase

Ostinato—a repeated melodic or rhythmic pattern

Slur—a curved line placed above or below two or more notes to indicate that they are to be performed smooth and connected

Tempo—the speed of the beat

Tie—a curved line connecting two notes of the same pitch and played as if they were one

Tie   Slur

PORTRAIT

Percy Grainger
(1882–1961)

An Australian composer, he lived from 1882 to 1961. His music is based on folk songs he collected from throughout the British Isles. He used a phonograph to record men and women singing the songs that were passed down to them from their parents and grandparents. In his arrangements of these folk songs for band, he tried to keep the phrasing as close to the original vocal performance as possible.

56 New Vistas

57 Claire de Lune CD :32

Folk Song, France

58 Mary With My New Notes

Traditional, U.S.A.

59 Los Pollitos CD :33

Folk Song, Ecuador

60 *When the Saints Go Marching In* CD :34

JAMES M. BLACK and
KATHERINE E. PURVIS, U.S.A.

61 **Catch a Falling Star** CD :35

Words and Music by
PAUL VANCE and LEE POCKRISS

62 **Sarasponda**

63 **Shepherd's Hey** CD :36

Country Dance, England

Band @ Home

LESSON 1

1. Complete "Mary With My New Notes" by notating the missing melody. We will play our completed song in our next lesson.

2. Practice playing "Claire De Lune" with the accompaniment track.

LESSON 2

1. Practice "Los Pollitos," "When the Saints Go Marching In," and "Catch a Falling Star" at different tempi.

2. Explain and play for someone at home the difference between a tie and a slur.

3. Revise "Mary With My New Notes" looking for:

   • Straight note flags
   • Neatly written note heads
   • Correct notes
   • Evenly spaced notes

4. Add the following to your composition:

   • New appropriate words
   • Dynamics

5. Be prepared to share your composition with the band.

LESSON 3

1. Create a one measure rhythmic ostinato to accompany "Mary With My New Notes".

2. Your ostinato should be on our first note (F) using any combination of quarter and eighth notes and quarter rests.

3. Remember that an ostinato is a repeated pattern.

Creative Tools of Music

> **Accent**—play the note with more emphasis

Chord—three or more tones sounded at the same time

Dot—increases the value of the preceding note or rest by one half

1st and 2nd Endings—play the first ending the first time only and the second ending the second time

 Time Signature—a symbol placed at the beginning of the staff with the top number indicating that there are 3 beats per measure, and the bottom number indicating a quarter note, which equals one beat

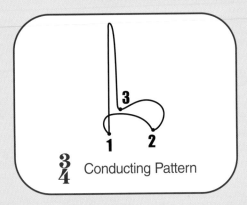

PORTRAIT

Gustav Holst
(1874–1934)

Gustav Holst was born in Cheltenham, England in 1874 and began composing while at Cheltenham Grammar School. While studying at the Royal College of Music, he met Ralph Vaughan Williams, another famous composer, and the two were close friends, always playing drafts of their newest compositions to each other. Holst was a teacher his whole life and because of a heavy and demanding teaching load, it took him many years to write his most famous work, "The Planets" (1914-1916). Despite his initial training at the Royal College of Music, Holst was largely self-taught as a composer, mostly learning by experience. He was an intense nationalist, and after his rejection from the Royal military because of his bad eyesight, he became a conductor of the military band, and toured much of Europe supporting the British through music. Some of his most well-known pieces include "Moorside Suite," "Suite in Eb," "Suite in F," and "The Planets."

64 Three at a Time

65 Batman Theme CD :37

Words and Music by NEAL HEFTI

66 Around Her Neck
She Wore a Yellow Ribbon

67 Shusti Fidli CD :38

Folk Song, Czechoslovakia

68 Change the Drum CD :39

**69 Oh Dear,
What Can the Matter Be?** CD :40

Folk Song, England/Scotland

70 In the Bleak Midwinter CD :41

GUSTAV HOLST, England

 Band @ Home

LESSON 1

1. After warming up properly, practice "Batman Theme" and "Around Her Neck."
2. Perform these songs for your family and friends. You may wish to ask your family if they remember "Batman Theme" from the classic television series.

LESSON 2

1. Explain 3/4 time to one of your family members.
2. Ask them to count for you as you play "Shusti Fidli."
3. Practice conducting each exercise before performing.

LESSON 3

1. Create and notate a new 8-count accent pattern. Be prepared to notate the pattern on the board during our next lesson for the band to play.
2. Practice "Oh Dear, What Can the Matter Be?" and "In the Bleak Midwinter."
3. Teach one of your family members how to conduct in a 3/4 time signature. Ask the family member to conduct as you play "Oh Dear, What Can the Matter Be?"

UNIT 12

Creative Tools of Music

Accidental—a sharp, flat or neutral, in a way not indicated in the key signatures

Concert pitch—the actual sounding pitch of a note played by an instrument

Introduction—a short section of music preceding the piece

Natural—this symbol cancels a previous sharp or flat sign; like a flat or sharp, it is used for the entire measure

Rock—a style of popular music that originated in America, characterized by a strong rhythmic beat and electronic instruments

Concert Pitch	F	D	E♭	B♭
C Instruments	F	D	E♭	B♭
B♭ Instruments	G	E	F	C
E♭ Instruments	D	B	C	G
F Instruments	C	A	B♭	F

Key of E♭

71 Song in E Flat

72 There's No One Exactly Like Me

By BETTY ANN RAMSETH

This Arrangement © 2003 Broadman Press   All Rights Reserved

73 March Flam CD :42

74 Happy Birthday to You! CD :43

Words and Music by
MILDRED J. HILL and PATTY S. HILL

mf

75 Jingle Bells CD :44

J. PIERPONT, U.S.A.

mf   *f*

76 Jingle Bell Rock CD :45

Rock!

Words and Music by
JOE BEAL and JIM BOOTHE

mf

77 Sunrise, Sunset CD :46

Lyrics by SHELDON HARNICK
Music by JERRY BOCK

f

mf

78 Hine Ma Tov CD :47

Folk Song, Israel

f   *mf*   *f*

Band @ Home

LESSON 1

1. Practice "There's No One Exactly Like Me" and "Happy Birthday to You!"
2. Perform "Happy Birthday to You!" for your family and friends.

LESSON 2

1. Practice "Jingle Bells" and "Jingle Bell Rock" alone and with the accompaniment tracks.
2. Memorize "Happy Birthday to You!"

LESSON 3

1. Practice playing long tones on the notes in your Concert Pitch Grid.
2. Practice playing concert pitches with a friend from band or while someone plays the concert pitches on the piano or keyboard.

Creative Tools of Music

Balance—the dynamic strength and importance given to instruments/voices within a composition

Multiple Measure Rest—a symbol indicating more than one measure of rest

Rehearsal Numbers/Letters—markings above the staff that indicate specific locations in the music

Sight-reading—the playing of a piece of music for the first time

Style—how notes, rhythms, and articulations are treated in musical performance

SIGHT–READING PROCEDURE MAP (SRPM)

1. Look at the title, composer, time signature, and key signature.

2. Look through the entire piece for the musical road map and for any key or time signature changes.

3. Follow along each line of music with your finger to be sure you know all of the notes and understand all of the rhythms and musical markings.

4. Count through the entire piece silently while tapping your foot.

5. Finger/airstick through the entire piece. Be sure to look at the words and symbols around the notes for all of the performance information.

6. Silently practice the difficult passages.

79 *Lotta Latin*

80 *Feliz Navidad*

Words and Music by JOSE FELICIANO
Arranged by MICHAEL STORY

81 Up on the Housetop CD :49

BENJAMIN RUSSELL HANBY, U.S.A.
Arranged by MICHAEL STORY

82 Rock Warm-Up

83 Winter Wonderland CD :50

Words by DICK SMITH
Music by FELIX BERNARD
Arranged by ROBERT W. SMITH

This Arrangement © 2003 WB MUSIC CORP.   All Rights Reserved

84 Holiday Warm-Up

85 *We Wish You a Merry Christmas*

Traditional, England
Arranged by ROBERT W. SMITH

86 **Dynamic Warm-Up**

87 **African Patapan**   CD :51

Carol, France
Arranged by MICHAEL STORY

88 **Concert Chorale**

Auld Lang Syne (Solo)

Traditional, Scotland

Jingle Bells (Solo)

J. PIERPONT, U.S.A.

Band @ Home

UNIT 13

LESSON 1

1. Practice "Feliz Navidad."

2. Warm-up slowly and carefully on long tones before each practice session.

LESSON 2

1. Practice "Feliz Navidad" and "Up on the Housetop," considering the style for each piece.

2. Remember to isolate the more difficult passages, playing them slowly and gradually increasing the speed.

3. Record yourself playing your part on "Feliz Navidad." Write down what you discovered from critically listening to yourself play.

Band @ Home

UNIT 14

LESSON 1

1. Review all three of the concert pieces, striving for individual improvement.

2. Make a recording of your performance of each piece and turn it in at our next lesson. Your teacher will review your recording and provide feedback for improvement.

LESSON 2

1. Review all of the concert pieces we have learned so far. If you are having difficulty with particular sections of a piece, play the section slowly to improve before going on.

Band @ Home

UNIT 15

LESSON 1

1. Review all of the concert pieces.

LESSON 2

1. Polish your performance on all of the concert pieces and prepare all music, equipment, and concert attire.

2. Tell your family and friends the reporting time and concert time.

3. Practice the solo pieces, "Jingle Bells" and "Auld Lang Syne," and perform them for your family and friends.

UNITS 16–18 WILL BE PRESENTED BY YOUR TEACHER

Creative Tools of Music

Allegro—fast tempo

Andante—slow (walking) tempo

Moderato—moderate or medium tempo

89 New Horizon Warm-Up

90 Finger Stretch

91 Marianne *CD :52*

Folk Song, Jamaica

Lively!

92 Scooby-Doo, Where Are You? *CD :53*

Words and Music by
DAVID MOOK and BEN RALEIGH

With energy!

93 Over There *CD :54*

Words and Music by
GEORGE M. COHAN

March

1.   2.

94 The Chicken Dance *CD :55*
(a/k/a Dance Little Bird)

By TERRY RENDALL and WERNER THOMAS

95 Walking Waltz

Andante

1.   2.

96 Moderato March

Moderato

97 Go, Go, Allegro!

Allegro

98 Can Can   CD :56   CD :57   CD :58

Andante/Moderato/Allegro

JACQUES OFFENBACH, France

99 Creative Expression

Band @ Home

LESSON 1

1. Practice "Marianne" and "Scooby Doo, Where Are You?" with the accompaniment CD.

2. Perform "Marianne" and "Scooby Doo, Where Are You?" for a family member or friend. Ask them if they have heard these songs before and if so where.

LESSON 2

1. Practice "Over There" and "The Chicken Dance."

2. Make up new appropriate motions to "The Chicken Dance" and teach them to someone in their family.

LESSON 3

1 Practice "Can Can" at Moderato, Allegro, and Andante tempi.

2. Explain the different tempi to one of your family members and perform "Can Can" at those tempi.

3. Create an 8-measure rhythmic composition on the staff provided and then apply the tempo markings you have learned in this lesson—Moderato, Allegro, and Andante. Perform your composition using a selected note.

Aaron Copland

(1900-1990)

Aaron Copland composed musical works for ballets, orchestras, choirs, and the movies. He composed "Billy the Kid" and "Rodeo," music based on American folklore. He also composed "Lincoln Portrait," which was a tribute to President Abraham Lincoln. One of Copland's best-known works is "Fanfare for the Common Man."

Key of F

E

F

100 Siren Warm-Up

mf

101 Great Granddad

Cowboy Song, U.S.A.

Allegro

mf

102 Git Along Little Dogies

Cowboy Song, U.S.A.

Moderato

mf *f* *mf*

103 Goodbye Old Paint

Cowboy Song, U.S.A.

Allegro

f

104 Shaker Hymn

Appalachian Folk Song, U.S.A.

Andante

mf

UNIT 20

Line 104 continued

105 *Five Foot Two, Eyes of Blue*

Lyric by SAM LEWIS and JOE YOUNG
Music by RAY HENDERSON

Allegro

106 **The Hey Song** CD :59

By MIKE LEANDER and GARY GLITTER

Rock

107 *New for a Few*

Andante

108 *Norwegian Mountain Dance*

Folk Song, Norway

Allegro

109 **The Merry Go Round Broke Down** CD :60

Words and Music by
CLIFF FRIEND and DAVE FRANKLIN

Allegro

110 *Creative Expression* **Complete the Composition Worksheet #13.**

Band @ Home

LESSON 1

1. Perform the three selections learned today, "Git Along Little Dogies," "Great Granddad," and "Goodbye Old Paint," for your family.

LESSON 2

1. Practice the new note we learned today, concert E.

2. Play "Shaker Hymn" for your family. Ask if they have heard this song before.

3. Tell your family that Aaron Copland used "Shaker Hymn" in his composition "Appalachian Spring."

4. Play "The Hey Song" with the accompaniment track.

LESSON 3

1. Perform, "Norwegian Dance", and "The Merry-Go-Round Broke Down" for your family and friends.

2. Complete Worksheet #13, "110 Creative Expression."

29

UNIT 21

Creative Tools of Music

Measure Repeat Sign—
a symbol that indicates to repeat the previous measure

Time Signature—
$\frac{2}{4}$ 2 beats per measure
Quarter note receives one beat

$\frac{2}{4}$ Conducting Pattern

Mariachi Cobre

111 *Back to Home*

Andante

mf

112 *Getting Even*

Moderato

mf

113 *Cucu Cucu*

Folk Song, Spain

Allegro

mf

114 *Cielito Lindo* CD :61

Folk Song, Mexico

Allegro

f

115 *Building the Long Tone*

Moderato

mf

116 *Eighth Rest Workout*

Moderato

1 + 2 + 3 + 4 +   1 + 2 + 3 + 4 +   1 + 2 + 3 + 4 +   1 + 2 + 3 + 4   1 + 2 + 3 + 4 +   1 + 2 + 3 + 4 +

mf

117 *Mi Caballo Blanco*

Folk Song, Chile

Moderato

mf

118 Rest on the Beat

Moderato

mf

119 El Juego Chirimbolo CD :62

Folk Song, Ecuador

Moderato

f

120 Relay Game

Andante

mf

121 San Sereni

Folk Song, Latin America

Moderato

mf

122 La Cucaracha

Folk Song, Mexico

Moderato

f

123 El Relicario CD :63

Folk Song, Mexico

Moderato

f

124 Creative Expression

Band @ Home

LESSON 1

1. Continue to practice, striving for the very best tone quality you can from your instrument.

2. Play "Cielito Lindo" and "Cucu Cucu" for your family and friends.

LESSON 2

1. Practice "Eighth Rest Workout" and "Rest on the Beat."

2. Play "El Juego Chirimbolo" for your family and friends.

LESSON 3

1. Practice "San Sereni," "La Cucaracha," and "El Relicario."

2. Continue to strive for the very best tone quality as you practice and perform.

3. On line 124 write a song using the following: 2/4 time signature, eighth notes and rest, repeat sign, and any of the pitches we have learned so far.

31

Creative Tools of Music

Legato—smooth and connected without interruption between the notes (soft start, long duration)

Staccato—play the note lightly and detached (light start, short duration)

Tenuto—play full value (long duration)

125 Theme From "The Surprise Symphony" CD :64

FRANZ JOSEPH HAYDN, Austria

Moderato

mf ... *f*

126 Song of the Volga Boatmen

Folk Song, Russia

Andante

mp ... *mf* ... *mp*

127 Paradiso CD :65

By ROBERT W. SMITH

Gently

mp legato

128 Smooth Sailing

Andante

mf legato

129 Dance of the Reed Flutes

Moderato

PETER ILYICH TCHAIKOVSKY, Russia

mf

130 The Long and Short of It

Moderato

mf

131 Sea Chanty CD :66

Allegro

Traditional Sea Chanty, England

mf

132 Can Can

Moderato

JACQUES OFFENBACH, France

f

133 Wipe Out CD :67

Moderate rock

By THE SURFARIS

f

Band @ Home

LESSON 1

1. Practice staccato articulations on all of the notes you have learned. It will take daily practice to train the muscles necessary to play articulations.

2. Warm-up slowly and carefully on long tones before each practice session.

3. Practice the "Surprise Symphony" with the accompaniment.

LESSON 2

1. Practice staccato and legato articulations on the notes you have learned. Practice slowly and carefully using the exact tonguing method needed for each articulation style.

2. Sight-read "Sea Chanty" as an example of legato and staccato style.

LESSON 3

1. Practice playing staccato, legato, tenuto, and slurs on each of the notes you have learned. Improvise with each articulation style on any exercise we have played so far and decide which articulation sounds the best. It will take daily practice to develop the muscles necessary to produce these varying articulations and styles.

2. Be sure to warm-up slowly and carefully on long tones or slow dexterity exercises before each practice session.

UNIT 23

Creative Tools of Music

Scenes of Daily Life in Korea, by Kim Junkeun

< Crescendo—gradually get louder.

> Decrescendo—gradually get softer.

Largo—very slow tempo

19ᵗʰ Century, ©Christie's Images Ltd. 1996

134 Louder and Softer

Andante

135 Ouma
CD :68

Mother Horse and Colt

Folk Song, Japan

Moderato

136 Sakura

Cherry Blossoms

Folk Song, Japan

Andante

137 Kaeru No Uta (Duet)

Folk Song, Japan

Moderato

138 Pentatonic Warm-Up

Moderato

34

139 Dots

Moderato

140 Ha'kyo Jung CD :69

Andante

Folk Song, Korea

141 Hua Gu Ge

Andante

Folk Song, China

142 Arirang

Andante

Folk Song, Korea

143 Dotted Note Warm-Up

Andante

144 Largo From "The New World Symphony"

Largo

ANTONÌN DVORÀK, Czechoslovakia

145 Crescent Moon

Moderato

Folk Song, China

146 Creative Expression Compose a pentatonic melody and ryhthm accompaniment on Worksheet #16.

Band @ Home

LESSON 1

1. Practice the pieces we played today, working to improve the articulations and crescendo and decrescendo. Practice slowly and carefully, remembering to use the exact tonguing method needed for each articulation style.

LESSON 2

1. Practice the "Pentatonic Warm-up" and "Arirang." Make a recording of both of these for review. Feedback on your progress will be provided.

2. You will turn in your recording of "Arirang."

LESSON 3

1. Practice and perform your favorite pieces of Asian music we studied this week.

2. Complete Worksheet #16, 146 Creative Expression.

3. Practice your composition and be prepared to perform for the class.

Creative Tools of Music

Da Capo (D.C.)—return to the beginning

Fine—the end

PORTRAIT

George Gershwin
(1898–1937)

George Gershwin's songs are some of the most lasting modern popular music written in the 20th Century. George Gershwin died when he was still fairly young. He is credited with being one of the first composers to merge jazz and classical music styles. One of his most famous works is the folk opera "Porgy and Bess."

147 *Low Tone Warm-Up*

mf

148 *Register Change Exercise*

mf

149 *Golden Gate March*

Moderato

mf   *f*

150 *'S Wonderful* CD :70

Flowing

Music and Lyrics by
GEORGE GERSHWIN and IRA GERSHWIN

1.   2.

mf

151 *Rhapsody in Blue™* CD :71

By GEORGE GERSHWIN

Flowing

mp

152 The Donkey Song
Traditional, U.S.A.

153 Summertime CD :72
By GEORGE GERSHWIN, DuBOSE and
DOROTHY HEYWARD and IRA GERSHWIN

Smoothly

154 I Got Rhythm CD :73
Music and Lyrics by
GEORGE GERSHWIN and IRA GERSHWIN

155 Creative Expression/Arrange and Notate

Arrange and notate on Worksheet #17.

 Band @ Home

LESSON 1
1. Practice "Rhapsody in Blue" and "'S Wonderful."
2. Practice your low notes and the "Register Change Exercise."

LESSON 2
1. Practice "Summertime" and "Donkey Song."
2. Practice your "Register Change Exercise."

LESSON 3
1. Practice "Summertime" and "I Got Rhythm" with the accompaniment tracks.
2. Complete Worksheet #17, 155 Creative Expression.

UNIT 25

Creative Tools of Music

Drum Circle—an interactive group of people gathered in a circle to play music on percussion instruments; a facilitator who directs the group in rhythm activities and improvised patterns usually leads a drum circle

Ritardando (Rit.)—gradually slow down

Syncopation—rhythm with the emphasis or stress on a weak beat or weak portion of a beat

Down	Up	(Down)	Up
1	**+**	**(2)**	**+**

Celebration, by Charles Searles (b. 1937)

©Smithsonian American Art Museum, Washington, D.C., Art Resource, N.Y.

156 You're a Grand Old Flag CD :74

GEORGE M. COHAN, U.S.A.

157 Hill and Gully CD :75

Caribbean

Folk Song, Jamaica

158 Cheki, Morena

Spirited!

Folk Song, Puerto Rico

159 African Warm-Up

Marilli

Gently

160 **Che Che Koolay** CD :76

Singing Game, Ghana

161 **The Rooster's Call**

Folk Song, Liberia

162 **Green Sally Up**

Folk Song, U.S.A.
D.C. al Fine

163 **Hello Lungile** CD :77

Folk Song, South Africa

164 **Lil' Liza Jane**

Words and Music by
COUNTESS ADA DELACHAU, U.S.A.

Band @ Home

LESSON 1

1. Practice "You're a Grand Old Flag" and "Hill and Gully" with and without the accompaniment tracks.

2. Create your own warm-up with syncopation and be prepared to share it with the band during our next class.

LESSON 2

1. Practice "Che Che Koolay" and "The Rooster's Call."

2. Describe a drum circle to several friends and/or family members and lead them in a drum circle performance. Find something resonant that sounds like a drum when played with your hands such as a box, can, or container.

LESSON 3

1. Practice "Green Sally Up" and "Hello Lungile."

UNIT 26

IS PRESENTED BY YOUR TEACHER

Creative Tools of Music

UNIT 26 IS PRESENTED BY YOUR TEACHER

Jazz—music rooted in improvisation and characterized by syncopated rhythms

𝄋 **Dal Segno (D.S.)**—repeat from the sign

Improvisation—the process of spontaneously creating a new melody

Swing—a style of jazz music characterized by the "lengthening" of the eighth notes that are on the beat

PORTRAIT

Edward Kennedy "Duke" Ellington
(1899-1974)

Duke Ellington is remembered as one of the greatest jazz artists and important composers of the Twentieth Century. He wrote thousands of compositions, which included jazz music, sacred music for the church, show music, and music for movies. Mr. Ellington composed jazz classics such as "It Don't Mean a Thing (If it Ain't Got That Swing)" and "Satin Doll." He was also a brilliant conductor, arranger, pianist, and bandleader.

165 **Gentle Warm-Up**

166 **Chorale**

167 **Angel Band**

African-American Folk Song, U.S.A.

168 Duke's Place CD :78
(a/k/a C Jam Blues)

Music by DUKE ELLINGTON
Lyrics by RUTH ROBERTS, BILL KATZ and ROBERT THIELE

Swing

mf

Ba - by!   Take me   down to   Duke's Place.   Wild-est   box in   town is

1.   2.

Duke's Place.   Love that   pi - ano   sound in   Duke's Place.

169 New Note Warm-Up

mp   *< mf*   *> mp*

170 Wade in the Water CD :79
Spiritual

African-American Spiritual, U.S.A.

1   (3) + +   1   (3) + +   1   (3) + +

mf

171 It Don't Mean a Thing (If It Ain't Got That Swing)

Words and Music by
DUKE ELLINGTON and IRVING MILLS

Fine   D.S. % al Fine

mf

172 Satin Doll CD :80

Music by DUKE ELLINGTON

Swing

1.   2.

mf

Band @ Home

LESSON 1

1. Practice "Duke's Place" with the accompaniment track.

LESSON 2

1. Practice "Wade in the Water" and "It Don't Mean a Thing (If It Ain't Got That Swing)."

2. Play long sustained tones on your new notes.

LESSON 3

1. Practice "Satin Doll."

2. Improvise your own four-measure song using the notes concert F, E♭, and D. Be prepared to perform your improvisation for the class at our next meeting. Use the provided accompaniment track on your student CD. **CD :81**

Creative Tools of Music

Half Step—the distance between two adjacent notes

Interval—the distance between two pitches

Scale—a stepwise progression used in melodies and harmonies

Whole step—a musical distance that equals two half steps

		W	W	H	W	W	W	H	
		1	2	3	4	5	6	7	8
Concert Key		B♭	C	D	E♭	F	G	A	B♭
C Instruments		B♭	C	D	E♭	F	G	A	B♭
B♭ Instruments		C	D	E	F	G	A	B	C
E♭ Instruments		G	A	B	C	D	E	F♯	G
F Instruments		F	G	A	B♭	C	D	E	F

173 There Are Many Flags in Many Lands   Traditional, U.S.A.

Flowing — mf

174 Oranges and Lemons   Folk Song, England

mf

175 Tinga Layo   CD :82   Folk Song, Jamaica

Calypso — mf

176 Concert B♭ Scale Warm-Up

half step   half step half step   half step

177 Chester   WILLIAM BILLINGS, U.S.A.

mf — f — mp — f

178 Peep Squirrel   CD :83   Folk Song, Africa

Mysterious — mf — f

179 Hao Peng You

Flowing

Folk Song, China

180 Kookabura

Folk Song, Australia

181 Ciranda   CD :84

Folk Song, Brazil

182 Over the Rainbow

Music by HAROLD ARLEN
Lyric by E.Y. HARBURG

Lyrical

Solo

Acc.

This Arrangement © 2003 METRO-GOLDWYN-MAYER INC. and EMI FEIST CATALOG INC.   All Rights Reserved

183 Creative Expression

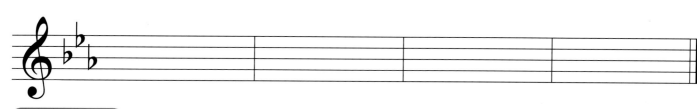

Band @ Home

LESSON 1

1. Practice the "sizzle" breathing exercise. How long can you hold the sustain?

2. Practice "Oranges and Lemons" and "Tinga Layo." Perform them for your family and/or friends.

LESSON 2

1. Practice "Peep Squirrel."

2. Practice and memorize the concert B♭ scale.

LESSON 3

1. Count and play "Kookaburra" and "Over the Rainbow." Some students will have the chance to perform "Over the Rainbow" as a solo in the next band class.

2. On the line provided (183), create your own eight measure composition, using the key indicated and the rhythms and pitches you have learned so far.

43

184 *Lip Slurs*

185 **On the High "C's"**

186 **Wabash Cannonball**

Traditional, U.S.A.

187 *Matchmaker*

Lyrics by SHELDON HARNICK
Music by JERRY BOCK

188 *Sleeping Beauty*

PETER ILYICH TCHAIKOVSKY, Russia

189 *"B" Your Best*

190 *Theme From Ice Castles (Through the Eyes of Love)*

CD :86

Music by MARVIN HAMLISCH
Lyrics by CAROLE BAYER SAGER

This Arrangement © 2003 EMI GOLD HORIZON MUSIC CORP. and EMI GOLDEN TORCH MUSIC CORP.   All Rights Reserved

191 **Concert C Major Scale**

192 **Santa Lucia**

Folk Song, Italy

193 **Doo Wah Diddy Diddy**

CD :87

Words and Music by
JEFF BARRY and ELLIE GREENWICH

194 **The Hey Song**

CD :88

By MIKE LEANDER and GARY GLITTER

Band @ Home

LESSON 1

1. Review the new note concert C you learned in this lesson.
2. Practice "Wabash Cannonball" and "Matchmaker, Matchmaker."
3. Ask your family and friends the name of the Broadway musical in which "Matchmaker, Matchmaker" was performed. ("Fiddler on the Roof")

LESSON 2

1. Perform "Theme from Ice Castles (Through the Eyes of Love)" for your family and friends. Ask if anyone has heard this song before and if so where.

LESSON 3

1. Practice the lip slurs introduced in class today. Be sure to make each note respond with the same quality and volume.

2. Perform "The Hey Song" in the new key for your family and friends.

3. On Worksheet #1, compose an 8-measure warm-up. You will have the chance to play this in class. This should contain some of the things we have discussed before that are contained in a good warm-up. This could include long tones, lip slurs, articulation exercises, and so on.

45

John Philip Sousa
(1854–1932)

Sometimes known as the "March King," John Philip Sousa wrote some of the most famous and recognizable marches in the world. Sousa was born in 1854 and he started studying music at the age of 6. When he was 13 years old his father enlisted Sousa in the Marines after he tried to run away from home to play in a circus band. In 1880, Sousa was appointed conductor of the United States Marine Band in Washington DC, which is known as "The President's Own." He later organized the Sousa Band and traveled the country presenting concerts with this organization. Throughout his illustrious career, Sousa wrote over 130 marches. In 1987, his "Stars and Stripes Forever" became th official march of the United States of America.

195 *More Lip Slurs*

196 *Caissons Go Rolling Along*   CD :89

EDMUND L. GRUBER

197 *Marines Hymn*

Traditional, U.S.A.

198 *Anchors Aweigh*   CD :90

Words and Music by
Capt. ALFRED H. MILES, U.S.N. (Ret.) and CHAS. A. ZIMMERMANN

199 *El Capitan*

Moderato

JOHN PHILIP SOUSA, U.S.A.

200 **The Thunderer**

Moderato

JOHN PHILIP SOUSA, U.S.A.

201 **Blow Away the Morning Dew**

Moderato

Folk Song, England

202 **The Yellow Rose of Texas** CD :91

Folk Song, U.S.A.

Moderato

203 **Na Na Hey Hey** CD :92

(Kiss Him Goodbye)

Words and Music by
GARY DE CARLO, DALE FRASHUER and PAUL LEKA

Allegro

Band @ Home

LESSON 1

1. Always warm up with long tones and strive for the best tone quality possible.

2. Practice "Caissons Go Rolling Along," "The Marines Hymn," and "Anchors Aweigh."

3. Ask your family members if they can identify which branch of the U.S. Armed Services these marches represent.

LESSON 2

1. Remember to start your practice session with the proper warm-up.

2. Teach your family and friends about the composer John Philip Sousa.

3. Play "El Capitan" and "The Thunderer" for your family and friends.

LESSON 3

1. Practice "Blow Away the Morning Dew," "The Yellow Rose of Texas," and "Na Na Hey Hey (Kiss Him Goodbye)."

2. As you practice these three pieces, remember to play with the best sound possible, with the correct note values, and with the proper articulations.

Johann Sebastian Bach
(1685–1750)

Johann Sebastian Bach was one of the most important composers in European history. He was a church musician all of his life and people today still regularly sing and play his music in church. He did not play the piano until he was an old man, so most of his keyboard music was composed for the organ or clavichord, a very popular keyboard instrument during the Baroque era. The Baroque era style included much ornamentation that was added to clothing, furniture, and architecture. Baroque music also was very ornamented.

204 Down and Up
Moderato

205 Manhattan Beach CD :93

JOHN PHILIP SOUSA, U.S.A.
Arranged by MICHAEL STORY

Moderate march tempo

209 Let Freedom Ring CD :96

Traditional
Arranged by ROBERT W. SMITH

Eine Kleine Nachtmusik

WOLFGANG AMADEUS MOZART, Austria

Over the Rainbow (Solo)

Music by HAROLD ARLEN
Lyric by E.Y. HARBURG

Music for the Royal Fireworks

GEORGE FRIDERIC HANDEL, Germany/England
Arranged by SANDRA DACKOW

Band @ Home

LESSON 1 & **LESSON 2**

1. Be sure to warm-up slowly and carefully on long tones before each practice session.

2. Review all of our concert pieces we have played so far.

3. Remember to isolate the more difficult passages, playing them slowly before gradually increasing the speed.

4. Make a recording of your performance of each piece and turn it in at our next lesson. Write down what you discovered from critically listening to yourself play. Your teacher will review your recording and provide feedback for improvement.

5. Practice the solos on page 50–51 "Over the Rainbow" and "Eine Kleine Nacht Musik," and perform them for family and friends.

UNITS 33-36
ARE PRESENTED BY YOUR TEACHER

51

Treasury of Scales: Concert B♭

Treasury of Scales: Concert E♭

Treasury of Scales: Concert F

Treasury of Scales: Concert C

FLUTE FINGERING CHART

UNIT 20

UNIT 13

UNIT 13

UNIT 13

UNIT 6

UNIT 6

UNIT 4

UNIT 4

UNIT 4

UNIT 20

UNIT 4

UNIT 10

UNIT 12

UNIT 10

UNIT 12

UNIT 29

UNIT 29

Glossary

Page numbers refer to the Student Book page where the definition is shown.

1st and 2nd Endings—*Play the 1st ending, repeat the section and play only the 2nd ending the second time. (18)*

Accent—*Play the note with more emphasis. (18)*

♯, ♭, ♮ **Accidental**—*A sharp, flat, or natural not indicated in the key signature. (20)*

Allegro—*Fast tempo. (26)*

Anacrusis—*One or more notes that come before the first full measure. (14)*

Andante—*Moderately slow (walking) tempo. (26)*

Articulation—*A slight interruption of the air stream with the tongue. (4)*

Balance—*All parts played and heard equally. The dynamic strength and importance given to instruments/voices within a composition. (10)*

Bar Line—*The vertical line placed on a staff to divide the music into measures. (4)*

❜ **Breath Mark**—*A recommended place to breathe. (4)*

Canon—*Music in which the melody is introduced in one voice and echoed by another voice. (8)*

Carol—*A song of praise or celebration. (–)*

Chorale—*A slow, "hymn-like" composition. (12)*

Chord—*Three or more tones sounded at the same time. (18)*

Clef—*A symbol placed at the beginning of the staff to identify the note names on the staff. (4)*

Common Time—*4/4 time signature. (–)*

Crescendo, Cresc.—*Gradually get louder. (34)*

Da Capo, D.C.—*Return to the beginning. (36)*

D.S.—Dal Segno—*Repeat from the sign. (40)*

Decrescendo, Decresc.—*Gradually get softer. (34)*

Dot—*Increases the value of the preceding note or rest by one half. (18)*

Duet—*A piece of music with two interacting parts. (10)*

Dynamics—*Musical performance levels of loud and soft. (14)*

Embouchure—*The natural formation of the facial and lip muscles on the mouthpiece or reeds. (4)*

⌢ **Fermata**—*Hold the note or rest longer than note value. (4)*

Final Bar Line—*Placed on the staff to indicate the end of a piece of music. (4)*

Fine—*The end. (36)*

♭ **Flat**—*A symbol that lowers the pitch of a note one half step. (4)*

Folk Song—*A song of cultural heritage passed from generation to generation sometimes through aural tradition. (–)*

𝆑 **Forte**—*Loud. (14)*

Grand Staff—*The Treble and Bass Clef staves joined together. (4)*

Half Step—*The distance between two adjacent notes. (42)*

Harmony—*The result of two or more tones sounded at the same time. (10)*

Improvisation—*Spontaneously creates a new melody without the intent to revise. (40)*

Interval—*The distance between two pitches. (4)*

Intonation—*The accuracy of pitch or pitch relationships in the performance of music. (6)*

Introduction—*A short section of music at the beginning of a piece. (20)*

Jazz—*Music rooted in improvisation and characterized by syncopated rhythms. (40)*

Key—*The tonality of a piece of music. (10)*

Key Signature—*Flats and sharps placed immediately following the clef used to indicate which notes are to be altered throughout the piece. (10)*

Largo—*A very slow tempo. (34)*

Ledger Lines—*Short lines placed above or below the staff for pitches beyond the range of the staff. (4)*

Legato—*Smooth and connected without interruption between the notes. (32)*

March—*Music for a parade or procession. (10)*

Measure—*The space between two bar lines to form a grouping of beats. (4)*

𝄎 **Measure Repeat sign**—*A symbol that indicates to repeat the previous measure. (30)*

Melody—*A series of musical tones that form a recognizable phrase to express a composer's thoughts or statements. (16)*

𝆐𝆑 **Mezzo Forte**—*Medium loud. (14)*